W9-CNK-144

NoLex 1/13

THE LIBRARY OF
AMERICAN
LIVES AND TIMES™

ABIGAIL
ADAMS

A Revolutionary Woman

Jacqueline Ching

The Rosen Publishing Group's
PowerPlus Books™
New York

To the women in my life,
especially Vivien, Betty, Juliana, Joyce,
Juliet, Julie, Maria, Alexandra, and Elizabeth

Published in 2002 by The Rosen Publishing Group, Inc.
29 East 21st Street, New York, NY 10010

First Edition

Editor's Note: All quotations have been reproduced as they appeared in
the letters and diaries from which they were borrowed. No correction was
made to the inconsistent spelling that was common in that time period.

Ching, Jacqueline.
Abigail Adams : a Revolutionary woman / Jacqueline Ching.
      p. cm. — (The library of American lives and times)
Includes bibliographical references and index.
ISBN 0-8239-5723-3 (lib. bdg.)
1. Adams, Abigail, 1744–1818—Juvenile literature. 2. Presidents'
spouses—United States—Biography—Juvenile literature.
3. Women—Suffrage—United States—History—Juvenile literature.
4. Adams, John, 1735–1826—Juvenile literature.
[1. Adams, Abigail, 1744–1818. 2. First ladies. 3. Women—Biography.]
I. Title. II. Series.
E322.1.A38 C48 2002
973.4'4'092—dc21

                                                            2001000255

Manufactured in the United States of America

CONTENTS

1. A Woman of Liberty

Abigail Adams lived in one of the most exciting periods of American history. Toward the end of the eighteenth century, she and her husband, John Adams, witnessed events that led to the birth of our nation. Eventually he became the second president of the United States of America, and she the first lady. John Adams is considered to be one of the Founding Fathers of the United States of America, because he was one of the delegates to the first Congress and a drafter of the Declaration of Independence.

Abigail Adams belonged to a family with a long tradition of public service, so she was in a good position to observe the historic events taking place. In her lifetime, a revolution was fought and won, a group of North American colonies became a nation, and a democratic system of government was built.

This portrait was painted by an unknown artist around 1786. It is attributed by some to Mather Brown. It is traditionally said to be Abigail Adams. Abigail lived a very unusual life for a woman of her time. She was independent and the intellectual partner of her husband, John.

Photo credit: Richard Walker

It was in Abigail Adams's nature to inquire into the world around her. Her thoughts and observations are documented in the letters and diaries she kept. Through her words, we can learn about the popular opinions of the day. They also show us that this first lady of the United States was a devoted daughter, wife, mother, sister, aunt, and friend. Her letters and diaries are considered important American literature.

Abigail Adams wrote many of her letters while sitting at this desk in her home in Braintree, Massachusetts.

Abigail Adams and her husband, John, were patriots. This means that they supported the independence of the American colonies from Britain. In the early eighteenth century, America consisted of thirteen colonies under British rule. The rest of the continent had been either colonized by Spain and France, or was left unexplored. The three European nations often fought over ownership of territories in the Americas. The disputes, or fights, also involved the Indians native to the land. Individual tribes sometimes formed alliances with the different colonies, while others simply fought for their freedom.

Born Abigail Smith on November 11, 1744, the daughter of Reverend William Smith and Elizabeth Quincy Smith was fortunate because intelligent and

This portrait of Abigail's father, Reverend William Smith, was created by Daniel Munro Wilson based on a lost painting by Gilbert Stuart. In the eighteenth century, ministers were often the most educated members of society.

influential people surrounded her all of her life. Abigail's father came from a long line of ministers. Her grandfather, John Quincy, was also an important man in the community. Quincy was the speaker of the House of Representatives who negotiated treaties with the Indians. Edmund Quincy, Abigail's great-great-grandfather, first came to America from England in 1633. He became an elected official.

Like most girls, Abigail and her two sisters, Mary and Elizabeth, were educated at home in Weymouth, Massachusetts. Their brother, William, was educated in a formal school and was expected to continue his education at Harvard. In spite of her own limited education, Abigail kept herself informed by reading books and exchanging letters with knowledgeable

Like most young girls of her time, Abigail was not expected to enter a profession like law, medicine, or the ministry and so she did not receive a formal education. However, Abigail read a great deal and found other ways of educating herself.

people. She read the Bible, history, sermons, philosophy, essays, and poetry and became one of the most well read women in America.

From an early age, Abigail chose friends who were as interested in reading and writing as she was. Later she became a lifetime friend to Mercy Otis Warren, a historian and playwright. Warren was one of the few women at that time to receive a formal education, the kind for which Abigail Adams longed.

Abigail Adams thought women had as much right as men to formal education. She became a strong advocate of education for girls and made sure that her only daughter, also named Abigail, received a good education (although she still did not attend a formal school). At the time, women were not supposed to work outside the home. Most of them married at a young age. Because of this, their education was limited to informal lessons in music, dance, and embroidery, and a little math and reading.

She educated herself about the issues of the day and formed her own strong opinions of them. After marriage, one of John and Abigail's regular habits was to read the *Boston Gazette* together. She also made use of her husband's library, in addition to reading newspapers and journals.

In addition to the role of women, slavery was another issue of the day that interested Abigail Adams. She felt strongly against it. Slavery had been part of the economy since ancient times, and when the first European explorers came to America, they brought with them slaves from Africa. However, in a land overflowing with revolutionary ideas, a growing number of intellectuals began to question whether the slave trade was moral, or even economic. On moral grounds, Abigail Adams agreed that slavery had no part in a new nation founded on the principles of freedom. She and John did not own slaves.

John and Abigail originally met in 1759, but it wasn't until two years later that they began a courtship. At twenty-seven, John was a lawyer and a graduate of Harvard College. She was nine years younger. Soon after their second meeting, Abigail and John began to

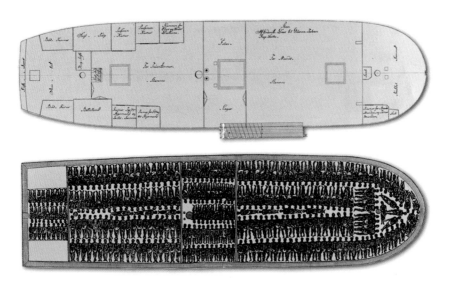

The slave trade to the Americas began as early as the sixteenth century. The capture of men, women, and children from Africa and their transportation to the New World lasted for more than three hundred years. A slave ship from the 1700s, as illustrated above, could hold hundreds of slaves and could travel great distances.

John Adams, pictured above, became the second president of the United States. John's father led a simple life as a farmer and a shoemaker, but the Adamses had deep roots in America. The family was part of the first generation of Puritan settlers in New England.

write to each other, and in these letters they became very close. Despite their different backgrounds, she became his "dear Partner in all the Joys and Sorrows, Prosperity and Adversity..." Thereafter, they would be each other's comfort and share in each other's trials and triumphs, mostly through letters. Her strong mind helped Abigail Adams to form a deep connection with her future husband. She fell in love with a man who had a different family background but who was her intellectual companion.

The Adamses were a working-class family, though well established and respected. John Adams inherited the house in which he was raised, in Braintree, Massachusetts, just 10 miles (16 km) south of Boston. He also inherited a barn, 10 acres (around 4 ha) of land, and 30 acres (12 ha) of orchard, pasture, and forest, also in Braintree. He and Abigail would raise their three sons and daughter there. Like Abigail, John also inherited a work ethic and strong values, which would come in handy during the times of political upheaval and personal strife.

This drawing was done by Elizabeth Susan Quincy in 1822. It is entitled *Birthplaces of John Adams and John Quincy Adams, Braintree, Mass.* It illustrates the connection John Adams had to the country. During his life, John would feel uncomfortable in cities and more at home on his farm.

John played a pivotal, or important, role during the American Revolution, as a delegate to the Continental Congress. The delegates had the difficult job of laying the foundations of the new country. They came up with two documents that still serve as the basis for our government today: the Declaration of Independence and the Constitution of the United States. Abigail Adams played her own part in the birth of the nation. She endured the hardships of the American Revolution with the knowledge that it was for the good of the country. She was a true patriot and used her mind and pen to promote liberty and democracy.

In her lifetime, Abigail Adams had opportunities to meet important statesmen and even become friends with them. Because of John's position in government, many of these statesmen visited her home and she took on the role of an excellent hostess. One of the government figures she met was Thomas Jefferson, who would become the third president of the United States, following John Adams. She kept up a long relationship through letters with Jefferson.

The Adams family sacrificed a great deal for their country. John's important role in Congress was not matched by a salary on which his family could adequately live. This put the family in hard financial times, especially after public duties forced John to give up his law practice once and for all. His duties with the Continental Congress, historic as they were, prevented

The U.S. Constitution was written by fifty-five men during the summer of 1787 to replace the Articles of Confederation. More than two hundred years later, the Constitution, along with the Bill of Rights, remains the central document guiding government in American life.

him from earning a living as a lawyer. He took cases when he could, but in 1778, he tried his last case. During one of John's absences, Abigail Adams realized that although they had been married for almost fourteen years, they hadn't been together for half that time. She felt that the "unfealing world" did not appreciate her family's sacrifice. Abigail worked as hard as her husband did to reshape the world they lived in, although her duties mostly kept her close to home.

2. The Pleasure of the Pen

In the eighteenth century, letters and diaries were the main literary forms, especially for women. Books were not widely available, although there were newspapers and pamphlets. Using quill pens, Abigail Adams wrote long, expressive letters and kept a diary, as did John.

Mail was the only method of communication with friends and family who were not close by. Abigail Adams wrote to many people, including her friend, Mercy Otis Warren, her sister, Mary Cranch, public officials who also befriended her, like Thomas Jefferson and James Lovell, and intellectuals like Catherine Sawbridge Macaulay.

Letters were of great importance to Abigail Adams. She wrote, "There are perticular times when I feel such an uneasiness, such a restlessness, as neither Company, Books, family Cares or any other thing will remove, my Pen is my only pleasure." Letters gave her an arena in which to explore her abundant ideas and exchange them with anyone who entered her life. She was able to express thoughts with pen and paper that she never would have spoken if the person were with her. "My pen is always freer than my tongue. I have written many things to you that I suppose I never could have talked," she wrote.

She often made literary and historic references in her letters, which reflected her level of education. The names of Alexander the Great, Caesar, and Polybus, the Greek historian, littered her correspondences. She shared an appreciation for contemporary writers of reputation, such as the French satirist, Molière, with Mercy Otis Warren, with whom she would share a lifetime of friendship and correspondence.

It was the custom of the time to copy formal letters from drafts. But usually first drafts were sent to close family. In a letter to her sister, Mary Cranch, Abigail Adams wrote, "My letters to you are first thoughts, without correction." She always asked people to destroy her letters. She was ashamed of her poor spelling. Luckily for historians, people ignored her wishes and countless letters have survived, allowing us to gain a firsthand perspective of life in Revolutionary America.

Outside of the close family circle, it was also the custom to address each other formally. For the length of their nearly fifty-year friendship, Abigail Adams and her friend, Mercy Otis Warren, addressed each other as "My dear Mrs. Adams" and "My dear Mrs. Warren." Mercy Warren and Abigail Adams began to correspond in the summer of 1773, after Abigail and John visited

This 1763 painting of Mercy Otis Warren was painted by John Singleton Copley. Mercy Warren was one of the most well known writers of the American Revolutionary period.

the Warrens in Plymouth. Mercy was the wife of John's friend, James Warren. Like the Adamses, the Warrens were patriots. Abigail Adams admired Mercy Warren, who was a prominent writer of the time and who struggled actively for the cause of women.

This is a close-up picture of Abigail's "Portia" signature. She borrowed the name from Shakespeare's Portia, an independent woman who dresses as a man so that she can be a more equal member of her society.

In their time, it was fashionable to sign letters using a pen name. These pen names usually were borrowed from characters in classical literature. In her youth, Abigail chose "Diana," the moon goddess of Roman mythology. After marriage, she sometimes signed her letters "Portia," a heroine from Shakespeare's play *The Merchant of Venice*. John was her "Lysander," named after a Spartan general. John also often called Abigail "Miss Adorable" in letters.

In the eighteenth century, the delivery of letters was a hazardous undertaking. The postal service was irregular, and during the Revolution, the postmaster general had to go into hiding from the British. Therefore, friends and relations often were counted on to carry letters and packages. John and Abigail Adams often relied on friends and family, such as Abigail's uncle, Cotton Tufts, a distinguished physician in

[To Abigail Smith]

II 2

LII 2

[4 Oct. 1762].

Miss Adorable

By the same Token
that the Bearer hereof satt up with
you last night I hereby order you
to give him, as many kisses, and
as many Hours of your Company
after 9 o'Clock as he shall please
to Demand and charge them to
my Account: This Order, or Requisition
call it which you will is in Consi-
deration of a similar order Upon Aurelia
for the like favour, and I presume I have
good Right to draw upon you for the Kisses
as I have given two or three Millions
at least, when one has been received and of
Consequence the account between us is
immensely in favour of yours

octr 4th 1762

John Adams

This is one of the early letters that John wrote to Abigail during their courtship. As in this letter that John addresses to "Miss Adorable," the letters between John and Abigail were often playful and affectionate, but they also discussed serious topics during the years of correspondence. John was so rarely at home that for years at a time their relationship was carried out solely through letters.

Weymouth, and even Thomas Jefferson, for this task.

There was always the danger that the letters would fall into unfriendly hands. While John Adams served at the Continental Congress, there were occasions when the British intercepted correspondence between Braintree and Philadelphia. For this reason, he requested that in her future letters Abigail "acknowledge the Receipt of all those you may receive from me, and mention their Dates. By this Means I shall know if any of mine miscarry."

The text to one intercepted letter, which he wrote to his wife in July 1775, emerged in the *Massachusetts and Boston Weekly News-Letter*, a conservative paper, giving him unwanted public attention. The original has never been found. In it he pondered the future of the colonies and the unique responsibility put upon the delegates: "When 50 or 60 Men have a Constitution to form for a great Empire, at the same Time that they have a Country of fifteen hundred Miles extent to fortify, Millions to arm and train, a Naval Power to begin, an extensive Commerce to regulate, numerous Tribes of Indians to negotiate with, a standing Army of Twenty seven Thousand Men to raise, pay, victual and officer, I really shall pity those 50 or 60 men."

Even if a letter was not intercepted, it could take weeks for it to arrive at its destination. While John Adams was in Europe, his letters to Abigail back home, and hers to him, often took months to be delivered.

There were other hazards for letters traveling across the ocean. They could be destroyed or lost if a ship hit bad weather.

For a period of ten years, from 1774 to 1784, John and Abigail Adams often were separated. This accounts for the frequency of their letters. They are firsthand accounts of how the couple worked as partners, but they also are filled with affectionate exchanges. They carried on much of their courtship through letters, and through them they shared their concerns and intimate thoughts. Their letters reveal a great deal of intimacy. Away from his fiancée, John Adams complained that "My soul and Body have both been thrown into Disorder, by your Absence, and a Month of two more would make me the most insufferable Cynick, in the World." For her part, her letters often referred to "loneliness" and "the too painfull Situation."

Not only did Abigail Adams write to John about their relationship and family matters, but she also wrote to him about what was happening in the colonies. She talked about how the people in Braintree were dealing with the arrival of the British soldiers. She told John, and the others she wrote to, how tense things were, how

In the eighteenth century, the mail often traveled slowly by horseback.

This portrait of John Adams by Benjamin Blyth was painted in 1766.
Ten years later, John had left his quiet life as a lawyer behind and
was serving the nation, far from his wife and children.

This portrait was painted by Benjamin Blyth about the same time as his portrait of John Adams (see page 23). Abigail missed her husband a great deal during his absences, but with her husband gone she took on many typically "male" responsibilities and became one of the most independent women of her time.

difficult it was to make ends meet. Paper money had become worthless and there were few men left to work the land. Abigail paints a picture for us, just as she did for John and her friends and relatives far away, of what life was like in Revolutionary America, and what it was like to be a woman living alone and caring for a large family.

3. Through Thick and Thin

When John and Abigail Adams were born, the United States of America did not yet exist. Massachusetts was still an American colony of Great Britain. At the time, Britain claimed sovereignty over thirteen colonies in America: Connecticut, Delaware, Georgia, Massachusetts, Maryland, New Hampshire, New York, New Jersey, Pennsylvania, Rhode Island, Virginia, North Carolina, and South Carolina.

John Adams's early career as a lawyer was only the training ground for the work that he would do later to help unite the colonies and form a new nation. At first, John Adams set up his law practice at home, turning a front room of their farmhouse into an office. His practice quickly grew. In 1764 alone, he had almost forty cases in Boston.

However, John Adams preferred life on the farm to the crowds of the city. Together with Abigail, he worked the land, plowing the fields and planting seeds. In 1765, she gave birth to their first child, also named Abigail. They nicknamed her Nabby.

This 1783 map was created after the Treaty of Paris was signed and the thirteen colonies had become states. During colonial times, each state thought of itself as a separate country. It wasn't until after the war against Britain that the states truly became united.

In the 1760s, John Adams set up his law practice at his farm. It would not be long before he would have to move into the city, though, as the political situation began to heat up between Britain and the colonies. Above is a photograph of his study which can be seen at the Adams National Historic Site in Quincy, Massachusetts.

These would be the last of their peaceful, domestic days for many years. John Adams soon would be drawn into the center of events that would shape a new democracy. In John's increasing absence, Abigail Adams took over more and more of the responsibilities around the farm. She also gave birth to four more children, John Quincy in 1767, Susanna in 1768, Charles in 1770, and Thomas Boylston in 1772. Susanna lived for only fourteen months. A sixth child, Elizabeth, was born dead in 1777.

In 1768, John Adams moved his family to Boston, where he could more easily practice law. Unfortunately the situation in Boston became increasingly tense, especially after the arrival of British soldiers in 1768. They effectively turned the city into a garrison. The turbulent times were difficult on John's law practice, as he explained in a letter to Abigail: "It is expensive keeping a Family here. And there is no Prospect of any Business in my Way in this Town this whole Summer.... We must contrive as many Ways as we can, to save Expences ...."

In the next four years, John Adams moved his family to Boston from Braintree twice. He often resolved to ignore politics, but in the end he could not ignore the

This engraving shows General Howe evacuating Boston during the American Revolution. General Howe was a Whig opposed to British actions against the colonies, but he obeyed King George III's orders and went to Boston to lead the British troops in the Battle of Bunker Hill, in June 1775. In March 1776, he evacuated Boston.

When British troops fired into a crowd in Boston, the event was widely publicized by patriots hoping to convince their fellow citizens to go to war against Great Britain. This famous engraving was created by Paul Revere to commemorate the event and to stir up the colonists against British soldiers in Boston.

events of the day. In 1770, John Adams tried a very important case. He was asked to defend a British captain and his men, who were charged with murder.

The incident took place on March 5, 1770, when a

wigmaker's apprentice taunted a soldier. The soldier then struck the apprentice on the head with the butt of his musket. When a hostile crowd gathered around them, the soldier called out for reinforcements. Captain Thomas Preston and six soldiers arrived on the scene, and a riot started. Five colonists were killed, and six were injured.

John Adams risked his reputation by accepting the case, but it was his belief that "Council ought to be the very last thing that an accused Person should want in a free Country." John won the case for the British, since it was uncertain whether the captain had ordered his soldiers to fire. All but two of the men, who were found guilty of manslaughter, were acquitted.

After the Boston Massacre, as it came to be known, Bostonians demanded the withdrawal of British troops. This was the first major clash between the Americans and the British, setting the wheels of the American Revolution in motion. It was a sign of how angry the colonists had become with British rule.

For the first half of the eighteenth century, Britain had been too busy fighting wars in Europe to care much about the colonies. But in 1763, Britain was finally at peace and King George III wanted to rule the colonies more actively. The French and Indian War in 1755, over disputed territories in America, burdened Britain with a large deficit. To raise money, the British Parliament began to pass a series of acts to tax the

This eighteenth-century painting of King George III was created by Thomas Gainsborough. During the reign of George III, Great Britain was involved in many wars in Europe and abroad. In an attempt to raise money for his armies, George passed taxes on the American colonists, turning them against Britain and speeding the call for independence.

colonies. The colonists, who had grown used to managing their own affairs, resented having to pay taxes to the mother country, as Great Britain was called. Many of them did not even feel that they were citizens of Great Britain, a distant country separated from them by the vast Atlantic Ocean. They felt that the colonists should rule themselves. These people became known as patriots. Those who still believed in remaining a part of Britain were known as loyalists.

This is a map of Great Britain from 1772. The colonists were beginning to wonder why they should be ruled by a government so far away, and one that clearly did not care about the issues that mattered to the people in America. Various acts to tax the colonies simply added fuel to the flame. Revolution was brewing.

When George III passed the Stamp Tax in 1765, citizens in Boston took to the streets in protest. In the background you can make out the image of a tax collector being hanged in effigy.

The Stamp Act, passed in 1765, was designed to pay for British troops in the colonies. It caused riots in Boston and New York City. Under the act, colonists were taxed on different kinds of printed matter, including newspapers, legal documents, and even items such as dice and playing cards. As a result of the Stamp Act, the courts and businesses were closed. John Adams had to halt his law practice, so he and Abigail needed to cut down on spending.

One year after the Stamp Act was passed, Parliament repealed it. This was followed by the Townshend Acts, which taxed articles imported by the colonies, such as lead, glass, paints, paper, and tea. Outraged, colonists began to consider larger issues, such as whether Britain had the right to tax them at all and the possibility of united resistance. John's cousin, Sam Adams, denounced the Townshend Acts and denied the authority of Parliament over the colonies.

The Tea Act, put into effect in 1773, was designed to help the struggling East India Company sell its excess tea in the colonies. It triggered a new burst of rebellion. "The flame is kindled and like Lightning it catches from Soul to Soul. Great will be the devastation if not timely quenched or allayed by some more Lenient Measures," Abigail Adams predicted.

On December 16, 1773, a group of colonists, disguised

This is a depiction of the reading of the Tea Act in New York City. Although tea was allowed into Boston Harbor, other port cities such as New York turned away ships bringing English tea to the docks.

Because of the Tea Act,
Abigail started serving coffee
rather than the more popular tea.
She also created "liberty teas"
by experimenting with sassafras,
sage, strawberry, raspberry,
and currant. Liberty teas became very
common at this time, as the colonists
resisted Britain's attempts
to control them.

as Mohawk Indians and shouting war cries, boarded three ships and dumped 342 chests of tea into Boston Harbor. None of the British sailors aboard were hurt, and the raiding party left the other cargo intact. The next day, John wrote in his diary, "Last Night, 3 Cargoes of Bohea Tea were emptied into the Sea.... This is the most magnificent Movement of all...."

Despite his moderate views, John Adams supported this action, known as the Boston Tea Party, which he saw as a necessary response to the British encroachment on American liberty. "The people should never rise without doing something to be remembered, something notable and striking. This destruction of tea is so bold, so daring, so firm, intrepid and inflexible, and it must have so important consequence, and so lasting, that I cant but consider it as an Epocha in History," he said.

In response to the Boston Tea Party, Parliament passed the Coercive, or Intolerable, Acts to punish the colonists. These acts closed the ports in Boston, limited the colonists' ability to meet, and placed several other harsh limits on their power. The colonists were outraged. The First Continental Congress was formed to

This 1856 color engraving, created by John Andrew, shows the Boston Tea Party of December 16, 1773. The Boston Tea Party was the beginning of the American colonists' resistance to British rule.

decide how the colonists should react.

This new epoch was the beginning of many long separations for Abigail and John Adams. They left Abigail Adams feeling very lonely. "The great distance between us, makes the time appear very long to me," she wrote to him. However, she was as much committed to his role in the country's birth as he was and wrote, "I long impatiently to have you upon the Stage of action...." She knew that the events unfolding were important and her loneliness was a necessary sacrifice.

4. Witness to a New Nation

Before the American colonies became a free nation, Americans had to fight a long and difficult war. The American Revolution went on from 1775 to 1783. In 1774, delegates from each of the colonies were sent to the First Continental Congress in Philadelphia, where they debated and decided what kind of nation America would be. John Adams and his cousin, Samuel Adams, were delegates from Massachusetts. Delegates from the other colonies included George Washington, Thomas Jefferson, John Hancock, Patrick Henry, Benjamin Franklin, John Jay, and Thomas Paine.

In 1775, John returned to Philadelphia as a delegate to the Second Continental Congress. While he was consumed by national issues, Abigail Adams

This hand-colored engraving shows the opening prayer of the 1774 Continental Congress in Philadelphia.

resigned herself to "much anxiety and many Melancholy hours." For her, the separations were the hardest part of the war. She wrote, "I had it in my heart to disswade him from going and I know I could have prevaild, but our publick affairs at that time wore so gloomy an aspect that I thought if ever his assistance was wanted it must be at such a time."

Despite missing her husband, she realized a war was unavoidable. She predicted: "It seems to me the Sword is now our only, yet dreadful alternative, and the fate of Rome will be renued in Brittain...When this happens the Friends of Liberty...will rather chuse no doubt to die [the] last of British freemen, than bear to live the first of British Slaves."

Two events occurred between the First and Second Continental Congress that launched the American Revolution. John Adams called these events at Lexington and Concord "the most shocking New England ever beheld." Immediately afterward, the Continental Congress authorized the creation of the Continental Army. In command of the army was General George Washington.

On April 19, 1775, British soldiers had set off from Boston to destroy the colonists' supply of arms in Lexington. Without this supply, the Massachusetts militia would be left defenseless. The arrival of the British regulars prompted the patriot Paul Revere to make his famous ride, shouting his legendary words,

Paul Revere became a legendary Revolutionary hero after he warned his fellow patriots about the arrival of British troops. His ride was immortalized in a famous ballad by the author Henry Wadsworth Longfellow.

"The British regulars are coming! The British regulars are coming!" In the course of the fighting at Lexington, the Americans lost eight men. However, they managed to repel the British soldiers 6 miles (9.6 km) down the road at Concord. John Adams worried that "the fight was between those whose parents but a few generations ago were brothers. I shudder at the thought, and there is no knowing where our calamities will end."

In the next serious battle of the Revolutionary War, Charlestown was "laid in ashes," but the rebels managed to capture some heavy cannon on Bunker Hill, overlooking Boston Harbor. Abigail Adams informed

This engraving was created by a Frenchman after the French had joined the fight for America's independence from Britain. The Battle of Lexington occurred on April 19, 1775, and officially began the American Revolution.

John of the events, calling it "The Day; perhaps the decisive Day is come on which the fate of America depends." She had just learned that Joseph Warren, a Revolutionary hero and close friend, had died in battle, and she prayed for the friends who remained in battle: "Almighty God cover the heads of our Country men, and be a shield to our Dear Friends. How [many ha]ve fallen we know not—the constant roar of the cannon is so [distre]ssing that we can not Eat, Drink or Sleep."

From her letters, John Adams learned about how the

battles were affecting their family and neighbors. He often read her letters to the other delegates to stress the plight of the nation. The destruction of Charlestown left many of them in difficult straits. Abigail Adams wrote, "Mr. Mather got out a day or two before Charlestown was distroyed, and had lodged his papers and what else he got out at Mr. Carys, but they were all consumed. So were many other peoples, who thought they might trust their little there..." Mather's papers were an invaluable collection of books and manuscripts. "The people from the Alms house and work house were sent to the [front] lines last week," she continued, "to make room for their wounded they say." Against their

This a painting by John Trumbull from 1786, entitled *The Death of General Warren at the Battle of Bunker's Hill, June 17, 1775*. Warren was a good friend of both Abigail and John, and his death helped them both realize how much independence from Great Britain might cost in human life.

mothers' wishes, John's brother joined the army, as had Abigail's brother.

When an epidemic of dysentery struck, Abigail Adams took charge of an ailing household. Their house was turned into a hospital for the sick and wounded. She wrote to John of "Soldiers comeing in for lodging," and "refugees from Boston tierd and fatigued…you can hardly imagine how we live." Her letter took more than a month to reach him. Four members of her family died from the disease: her mother, her cousin, John's brother Elihu, and Elihu's youngest child.

Political friends of John's sometimes visited the Adams home, and Abigail learned to act as hostess to them. These early social events prepared her for her future role as the wife of a vice president who would become president. On October 27, 1775, she was invited to dine with the journalist, scientist, and statesman Benjamin Franklin. Franklin was ahead of his time in his support of women's rights. Abigail Adams praised him in a letter to her husband. "I found him social, but not talkative, and when he spoke something usefull droped from his Tongue; he was grave, yet pleasant, and affable."

Abigail Adams felt the hardship of being without her husband was her patriotic duty and she occupied herself with wartime news and ideas. After the Boston Tea Party, Abigail Adams eloquently expressed her concerns for her countrymen in a letter to Mercy Otis

This portrait of Benjamin Franklin was painted in 1789 by Charles Wilson Peale. Franklin believed strongly in the equal rights of women and became one of Abigail's good friends. However, Benjamin Franklin and John Adams did not get along very well. Franklin thought of John as a poor farmer without good manners. John thought Benjamin was a snob.

Warren. "Altho the mind is shocked at the Thought of sheding Humane Blood, more Especially the Blood of our Countrymen, and a civil War is of all Wars, the most dreadfull Such is the present Spirit that prevails, that if once they are made desperate Many, very Many of our Heroes will spend their lives in the cause."

Abigail Adams knew that there was far more at stake than fighting against taxes: "The Building up a Great Empire, which was only hinted at by my correspondent may now I suppose be realized even by the unbelievers. Yet will not ten thousand Difficulties arise in the formation of it?...if we seperate from Brittain, what Code of Laws will be established. How shall we be governd so as to retain our Liberties? Can any government be free which is not adminstred by general stated Laws? Who shall frame these Laws? Who will give them force and energy?"

On July 4, 1776, the Continental Congress proclaimed the existence of a new nation, the United States of America, in the Declaration of Independence. John Adams, one of the signers of the Declaration, shared the excitement of the most significant day in American history with his wife: "I am apt to believe that it will be celebrated, by succeeding Generations, as the great anniversary Festival....It ought to be solemnized with Pomp and Parade, with Shews, Games, Sports, Guns, Bells, Bonfires and Illuminations from one End of this Continent to the other from this Time

In CONGRESS, July 4, 1776.

The unanimous Declaration of the thirteen united States of America.

John Adams originally was chosen to write the Declaration of Independence but decided to give the job to his friend Thomas Jefferson. Adams believed that Jefferson was the better writer.

Benjamin Franklin, Thomas Jefferson, John Adams, Robert Livingston, and Roger Sherman are shown working on the Declaration of Independence, in an undated engraving. The political philosophy of the Declaration had already been expressed by philosophers like John Locke. It simply summarized these ideas and listed complaints against the King to justify breaking the ties between the colonies and England.

forward forever more." However, he was also aware of the "toil and Blood and Treasure, that it will cost Us to maintain this Declaration, and support and defend these States."

While such momentous events took place, Abigail Adams continued to deal with the pressures of everyday life. She had to make decisions about financial matters and the welfare of her children without the benefit of her husband's guidance.

5. Life on the Home Front

Abigail Adams was a typical woman of the eighteenth century in that she saw her primary responsibilities as those of a wife and mother. She was uncommon in that circumstances forced her to become the primary decision-maker for her family. She approached each task in a practical manner, with hardly a complaint. For the ten years in which John was mostly absent, she managed not only the household but the farm and other business affairs.

Before the Revolution, John Adams supported his family with his law practice and income from his farm, which was rented in parts to tenant farmers. Once the Revolution began, he could no longer practice law, and the only income came from the farm and what little John could spare from his meager salary from

---

This portrait shows Abigail Adams in her twenties and is based on the portrait by Blyth. Though Abigail Adams was very independent, she was comfortable in her domestic role as wife and mother. She once wrote, "I believe nature has assigned to each sex its particular duties and sphere of action and to act well your part, 'there the honor lies.'"

> *Tenant farmers were people who did not own the land on which they lived. They had to pay rent to landowners for the use of the land they farmed. It was common for landowners to use tenant farmers to help work their land. The tenants paid rent either in cash or with a portion of the product they grew. Today tenant farmers make up about two-fifths of the world's farmers.*

Congress. In her husband's absence, Abigail Adams had to handle the daily problems of running the household. She always managed to make ends meet.

The farming business was not easy. There were crop failures, challenges of raising farm animals, and shortages of labor. Following John's advice, Abigail Adams put to work those tenants who were late on the rent. Later she hired some of them as laborers. The Adamses were never rich, but they managed to employ servants, as well as farmhands. Abigail was responsible for hiring all the help, which could be difficult, especially in times of inflation.

These are depictions of Continental Bills that were used as money after the American Revolution.

The value of money dropped greatly during the Revolution. It was up to Abigail to find ways to support her family in the middle of rising inflation and food shortages. Bread, meat, sugar, coffee, and cotton wool were in short supply, available only at very high prices. Abigail Adams wanted to free John from domestic worries so that he could focus on matters of government. Abigail avoided giving her husband details of her day-to-day problems, but wrote of these hard times to him, "Our Money is very little better than blank paper."

Always resourceful, Abigail Adams learned to live frugally and to make what her family needed, such as soap and clothes. She felt that this hardship was her patriotic duty to her country and took it all in stride. However,

This is a painting of colonial citizens shopping at a dry goods shop.

doing without material things was not enough to keep her family going.

As a mother, Abigail Adams took her duties seriously. She wrote to Mercy Otis Warren that "I am sensible I have an important trust committed to me; and tho I feel my-self very uneaquel to it, tis still incumbent upon me to discharge it in the best manner I am capable of."

Abigail raised her children with the hope that they might follow their father in leadership. Both she and John placed these hopes on their eldest son, John Quincy, in particular. He traveled to Europe with his father and began his political life at a very young age.

This is a portrait of the young John Quincy Adams by the artist Sydney L. Smith. John Quincy was educated in politics at an early age as he accompanied his father on many of his travels.

For all of their children, their main concern was their religious development. This was so important to Abigail that she wrote to John Quincy, after he left for Europe, that "I had much rather you should have found your Grave in the ocean you have crossd or any untimely death crop you in your Infant years, rather than see you an immoral profligate or a Graceless child."

From the beginning, John Quincy was destined to follow his father into politics. While in

Europe with their father, both John Quincy and Charles attended good schools, including the public school of Amsterdam and the University of Leyden. There they studied Greek and Latin. It was also important for John Quincy to study oratory and poetry, and to improve his writing skills. Abigail Adams urged her eldest son to "practise those Virtues which tend most to the Benefit and Happiness of Mankind."

John Quincy began to work at an early age. He was only fourteen when he started to work as secretary and translator for the U.S. envoy to Russia. Later he became his father's secretary in London.

John and Abigail Adams also focused on the education of their eldest child, Nabby. As a girl, she would have a different education than that of her brothers, but her parents wanted her education to go beyond music and dancing. Nabby would learn French, as her mother had, in addition to reading and writing.

This drawing shows an external view of Leyden University, founded in 1575 by William of Nassau.

Later in life, Abigail Adams was entrusted at various times with the care of her nieces and grandchildren. She always placed their interests above her own, as she had with her own children.

This is a portrait of Reverend William Smith by John Singleton
Copley. Reverend Smith, Abigail's father, was one of Weymouth's
most prosperous and well-educated citizens. He was easygoing and
friendly. Abigail later recalled that he often advised her to speak
kindly, both to people and about them, teaching her "to say all the
handsome things she could of persons, but not evil."

In 1778, Abigail sent Nabby to spend the winter at the home of her friend, Mercy Otis Warren, in Plymouth. In spite of her own loneliness—her husband and eldest son had recently left for France—she wanted her teenage daughter to benefit from the company of her talented and ambitious friend.

Unfortunately, Nabby would end up in an unhappy marriage to her father's secretary, William Smith. Her father had disapproved of her original suitor, Royall Tyler. Nabby's death in 1814 was an extremely painful loss for Abigail Adams, who always had a close relationship with her.

As for her sons, Abigail Adams could rejoice in Thomas, her youngest son, who became a lawyer, and John Quincy, who eventually became the sixth president of the United States. However, Charles, who began as a promising lawyer, became an alcoholic. He died prematurely at the age of thirty.

6. On Her Own

In 1778, toward the end of the Revolution, John Adams was sent to Europe on a diplomatic mission. He was elected to be joint commissioner to France, along with Benjamin Franklin and Arthur Lee. He brought John Quincy with him.

During this time, Abigail Adams sometimes went without a letter from him for months. Lonely and upset, she began to doubt their marriage and berated him for not writing. John was not always sympathetic during this time. Once again he worried that his wife's intimate letters might be intercepted and printed in the newspapers. He wrote: "It would be an easy Thing for me to ruin you and your Children by an indiscreet Letter—and what is more it would be easy, to throw our Country into Convulsions."

Abigail Adams also was discouraged by the new

Right: This is a map of France from around 1778, the same time that John Adams was sent to Europe as joint commissioner of France. France had been very helpful in the American Revolution, sending troops and supplies to help the colonies gain their independence from Britain. In the 1780s, France would fight a revolution of her own, trying to win more rights for the people.

THE

POST ROADS
OF
FRANCE,

from the Map of JAILLOT.

Published by Order of the

DUKE DE CHOISEUL,

Post-master general of that Kingdom.

LONDON:

Printed for Robt Sayer, No 53 in Fleet Street,
as the Act directs 2 March 1771.

developments of the war. Although the French recently had declared war with Britain in support of the Americans, the fighting in the north was at a stalemate. It would be another two years before the British would surrender at Yorktown. Abigail wrote to John, "And does my Friend think that there are no hopes of peace? Must we still endure the Desolations of war with all the direfull consequences attending it? —I fear we must and that America is less and less worthy of the blessings of peace."

Despite her concerns, Abigail Adams did not have much time to feel sorry for herself. She still had children at home to care for. She nursed her son Tommy and one of the servants through sickness. She also filled her days with charity work, attending church, visiting family and friends, reading, and writing letters.

Money continued to be a problem. Abigail Adams had to earn money to supplement John's small income in the face of inflation. The taxes on the farm were a large sum. She lamented to John of how money "depreciates in proportion to our exertions to save it."

First she decided to lease the farm to support her family. She saw another opportunity to make money by asking John to send her goods from Europe, which she then could sell. Accordingly, John sent her fans, bowls, china cups, ribbon, chintz, thread, and handkerchiefs. She achieved her goals of selling the merchandise and keeping the family going.

This is the rose china that Abigail Adams had made for her in Europe. She arranged for John to send her many items that she could not buy during the hard times of the American Revolution.

In another show of her independence, Abigail Adams bought a house in Vermont, where she and John could retire. Although women did not have the right to buy property, Abigail Adams was able to make several purchases in John's name. He did not respond to her letters on the subject, so she made her own decision to buy 1,620 acres (656 ha) of land in Vermont. John was not happy with her decision because he had no plans to retire in such wilderness. Abigail hoped that the town next to the land she had purchased would grow.

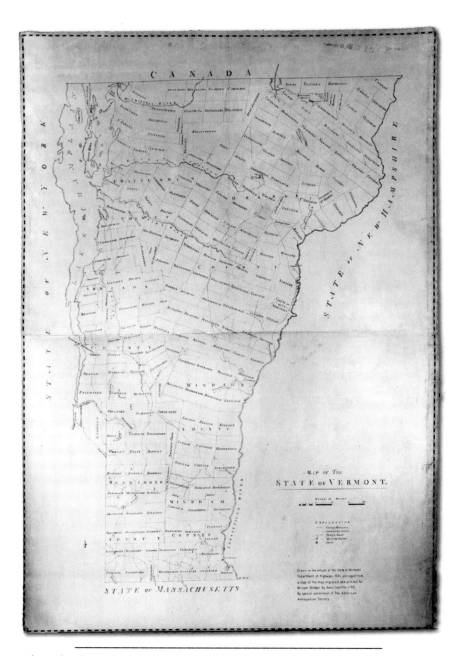

Abigail Adams bought a large piece of land in Vermont, hoping that she and John might retire there when he returned from Europe. John was not pleased with her purchase, but there was not much he could do from across the ocean.

Unfortunately her hopes were not realized. Abigail had to make other decisions without her husband, including whether to buy more property in Braintree and whether to sell their house in Boston.

John Adams returned home in 1779, but his visit was brief. He soon accepted a double commission from Congress to be the American peace commissioner and to negotiate a treaty of commerce with Britain. At the end of the year, he left again for France, this time with his two sons, John Quincy and Charles. "My habitation, how disconsolate it looks!" wrote Abigail, soon after their departure.

This time, she and John Adams were separated for five years, the longest separation of their marriage. Abigail was desperate when no letter arrived for nine months during this time. Although she knew the letters probably had been lost at sea, it didn't help. She was reunited with Charles when he returned home in 1781.

7. Abigail and John Abroad

The original purpose of John's second trip across the Atlantic was to negotiate peace with Britain. But his commission was extended again and again. Abigail Adams wrote to him, "How lonely are my days? How solitary are my Nights? Secluded from all Society but my two Little Boys, and my domesticks..." When the American Revolution ended in 1782, and John still was not expected to come home, Abigail Adams began to wonder whether to visit him in Europe or continue to wait for his return. In September 1783, the Treaty of Paris was signed, formally ending the eight-year American Revolution, and soon after, John Adams sent his wife an invitation to join him. In 1784, she sailed to England to join her husband and eldest son, accompanied by Nabby, who was nineteen years old.

Long before this, Abigail Adams had written to her cousin, Isaac Smith Jr., of her desire to travel, and in particular to see England: "From my Infancy I have always felt a great inclination to visit the Mother Country as tis call'd and had nature formed me of the

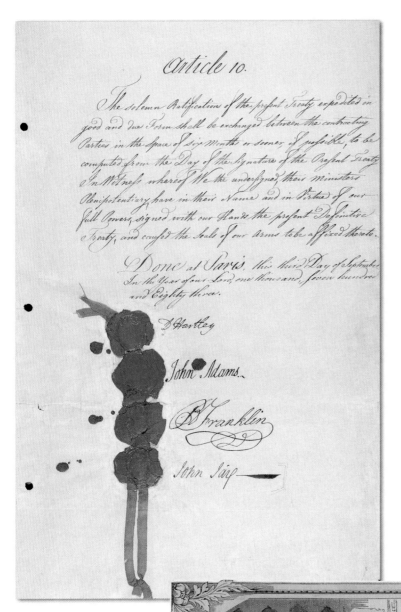

Article 10.

The solemn Ratifications of the present Treaty expedited in good and due Form shall be exchanged between the contracting Parties in the Space of Six Months or sooner, if possible, to be computed from the Day of the Signature of the present Treaty In Witness whereof We the undersigned, their Ministers Plenipotentiary have in their Name and in Virtue of our full Powers, signed with our Hands the present Definitive Treaty, and caused the Seals of our Arms to be affixed thereto.

Done at Paris, this third Day of September In the Year of our Lord, one thousand, seven hundred and Eighty three.

D Hartley

John Adams.

B Franklin

John Jay

The Treaty of Paris was actually a collection of treaties concluding the Revolutionary War and signed by Great Britain, the United States, France, and Spain. In the treaty, Britain recognized the independence of the United States with boundaries to the Mississippi River to the West and Canada to the North.

Right: This picture shows the signing of the Treaty of Paris.

This map of Europe was created in 1780. During the eighteenth century, the continent of Europe would host a number of different wars involving Spain, France, Germany, Great Britain, and Russia. Treaties signed by these nations often would rewrite old maps, creating new boundaries. This sometimes led to new conflicts.

other Sex, I should certainly have been a rover."

Her decision to travel abroad was not an easy one. She would be gone from home for a long time, and in her absence many things would change. The trip from Boston to England alone would take one month. She found the ocean voyage "formidable." By the time she returned, the sons she left behind, Charles and Tommy, would be grown. She also did not expect to see again her elderly mother-in-law, who had been her closest neighbor. She feared she was "unequal to the trial." In the end, she followed "the most earnest wish of my Soul," which was to be with her husband.

In the months before her departure, Abigail Adams had many preparations to make. She left the house in the care of a servant, Pheby, and the farm with a longtime tenant. She left other financial matters to the attention of relatives. She decided to leave her youngest sons with her sister Betsy Shaw, under whose care they would attend a "very good School." Betsy often took in boarders and tutored children for extra money. All of Abigail Adams's sons were prepared for Harvard there. Abigail had to say emotional good-byes to family, friends, and neighbors before her trip. Finally she closed her home and hired two servants to accompany her and Nabby on their journey.

At the end of May 1784, Abigail Adams wrote to John that she had bought passage on the ship, *Active*, adding her estimated date of arrival in London. She was in England before the letter reached him. The

journey across the Atlantic Ocean was a rough one. Several passengers, including Abigail Adams and her daughter, suffered from seasickness. Abigail was also bedridden with fever and pain from rheumatism, which she blamed on the damp air.

When Abigail and Nabby Adams arrived in London, they discovered that John Quincy had been waiting for them in London for a month, but he had gone back to The Hague, in the Netherlands, just days before their arrival. John was also in The Hague on official business. He sent John Quincy right back to London and followed a week and a day later. The last time Abigail Adams had seen John Quincy, he was only twelve years old. At that time, he was seventeen. "We are indeed a very very happy family once more met together after a Separation of four years," wrote Abigail to her sister Mary Cranch.

This is a photograph of part of an English Gothic cathedral. Abigail Adams did not like the Gothic style of architecture, finding it oppressive.

Abigail Adams wrote vivid and detailed accounts of her travels to her sisters and nieces back home.

Left: This drawing by J.R. Wells is called *Homeward Bound.* It shows a typical ship of the time sailing on rough seas. Traveling by sea in colonial times was not easy. It could take months, and weather was often severe. Abigail Adams suffered severe seasickness on her voyage.

This photograph of the Adams family residence in France
taken in 1920 by Fernand Girardin is entitled
Maisons de Plaisances, Parces et Jardins.

The old Gothic cathedrals of Canterbury had "a most
gloomy appearance and realy made me shudder." In
Blackheath Forest, on the way to London, they witnessed a robbery. When she saw that the robber was a
youth about twenty years old, she was saddened by his
fate, which in England in those days was death by
hanging.

After London, John Adams was posted to France and
the family rented a mansion just outside Paris. It was
close to where another American minister, Benjamin

This portrait of Thomas Jefferson was done by Gilbert Stuart between 1805 and 1807. This portrait is considered by many to be the finest existing image of the third president of the United States, made during his second term in office. Unlike depictions of lavishly dressed royal rulers, Stuart portrays Jefferson dressed in sober black and possessed of a presence and authority independent of wealth.

Franklin, was living. The mansion, with its 5 acres (2 ha) of garden, were grand, but had been neglected. Abigail Adams had to put a lot of work into fixing it up, and with little money. John's position as a minister paid very little, and Paris was expensive. He even had to borrow money from banks for himself and Franklin.

Although Abigail Adams had studied the French language as a child, she was uncomfortable speaking it, which limited her exploration of the country. The only person she became friendly with was Thomas Jefferson, who was "one of the choice ones of the Earth." He respected her highly as a woman of taste and insight. Sometimes she and her son or daughter would go into the city with Jefferson to a concert, play, or some other activity.

Nevertheless, the language barrier and strangeness of French customs made her feel homesick, and she wrote to Mary Cranch, "No severer punishment need be inflicted upon any mortals than that of banishment from their Country and Friends." Luckily for Abigail Adams, they would live in France for only ten months, as Congress had appointed John a minister to Britain.

John Quincy, who had been accepted at Harvard, left for Boston at the same time that his parents left for England. London suited the Adamses better. They settled into a large house on Grosvenor Square and a lifestyle that befitted a foreign minister. They had distinguished neighbors, including the British foreign

This is a south-facing view of modern-day Grosvenor Square and Oxford Sreet in London. John and Abigail Adams lived on Grosvenor Square while John was minister to Britain.

minister, dukes, and duchesses. Abigail Adams enrolled in a series of lectures on natural science.

Their arrival in London also marked the beginning of a frequent exchange of letters between Abigail Adams and Thomas Jefferson. They also exchanged small favors. When Jefferson's daughter, Polly, came to visit him in France, he asked that she travel through England to enjoy Abigail's hospitality.

However, the British were still hostile to American visitors. John Adams found them unwilling to negotiate, making it difficult for him to achieve his purpose, which was to agree on the British evacuation of western outposts and the settlement of American debts to British creditors.

To Abigail Adams's further dismay, Congress had decided to reduce John's income, in spite of the fact that their expenses were even greater in England than they had been in France. Nevertheless, they made the best of their circumstances. Eventually John was frustrated with the uselessness of his presence in London and sent Congress his resignation. In 1788, the Adamses sailed home to Massachusetts.

8. America's First Lady

In 1789, America's political leaders were struggling to form a government worthy of the blood that had been shed during the Revolutionary War. In that year, an American electorate voted in the first president of the United States, George Washington, the hero of the Revolution. Washington selected John Adams to be his vice president. Thomas Jefferson later would be appointed secretary of state.

Because Congress had not arranged for their housing, John needed Abigail's help to set up a residence in New York, which at the time was the nation's capital. The Adams family could not afford to rent a furnished house on a John's salary, so

This painting depicts the morning of the first Inauguration Day in 1789 in New York City. George Washington would be elected first president of the United States by a unanimous vote.

This is a 1796 portrait of George Washington by Gilbert Stuart. Adams served as the first vice president of the United States in Washington's administration. During that time, the vice president had very few duties, and John thought of the position as one of the most purposeless jobs ever created.

Abigail Adams was supposed to bring linen, silverware, and furniture with her from home. John wanted her to hurry to New York, but she did not want to move until she knew there was a house to move into.

In the meantime, she had so much work around the farm to finish, from selling extra livestock to ordering hay, that she lost sleep from worry. She had arranged for John's brother to take over the farm, but that fell through.

Finally Abigail Adams made it to New York. For two years, she enjoyed life in their Richmond Hill house, from which they could watch ships sail up and down

This is a 1790 engraving by Cornelius Tibout of the Richmond Hill home of John and Abigail Adams. The Richmond Hill mansion, built in 1767, was one of New York's most impressive structures. Set on a hill near the Hudson River, it provided a panoramic view of the city, and of neighboring New Jersey and Long Island.

This is a portrait of First Lady Martha Washington, who was one of Abigail's closest friends.

the Hudson River. The house, set in a rural area, was "convenient for one family, but much too small for more," as she described to her sister Mary. It was "not in good repair."

Abigail Adams became a good friend to Martha Washington, the president's wife. She described the first lady in a letter to Mary: "She is plain in her dress, but that plainness is the best of every article...Her hair is white, her Teeth beautifull, her person rather short than otherways...Her manners are modest and unassuming, dignified and fememine..." As for George Washington, she found him to be a mix of formality and graciousness that "creates Love and Reverence."

As the wife of a vice president, she had many social duties. She scheduled weekly receptions on Monday nights and held formal dinners for members of Congress on Wednesdays. She had to return formal visits and organize parties. "The New Years day in this state, & particularly in this city is celebrated with every mark of pleasure and satisfaction," she wrote to Mary about the New Year's celebration of 1790. "The V.P. visited the President & then returned home to receive His Friends." That

Abigail and John spent a great deal of time entertaining
foreign dignitaries and heads of state during his time in office.

evening she received many guests in her drawing room,
all "Brilliantly drest, diamonds & great hoops ecepted."

Eventually she became bored with this routine,
which she described to Mary: "Servants & Gentlemen
and Ladies...come out to make their Bow & Curtzy,
take coffe & Tea, chat an half hour, or longer, and then
return to Town again." Abigail Adams wondered if
being the vice president's wife was worth the trouble
and expense. She found it difficult to obtain servants
with proper manners to help her run the household.
"My Housekeeper who on many accounts has been the
most Respectable Female I have had in the Family, is so
sick and infirm that she is obliged to leave me..."

To Abigail Adams's dismay, she had to leave New York, where she had been close to Nabby and her children. Congress had debated where to establish a permanent capital and settled on Philadelphia, for the time being. The Adamses moved there in September 1790. Abigail Adams liked their new house, which had beautiful views, better than the one in New York. However, she had the same problem finding suitable servants, because "most of them [were] drunkards."

Through their first winter in Philidelphia, Abigail Adams was seriously ill. The following spring, she went back home to Braintree, now called Quincy, after her

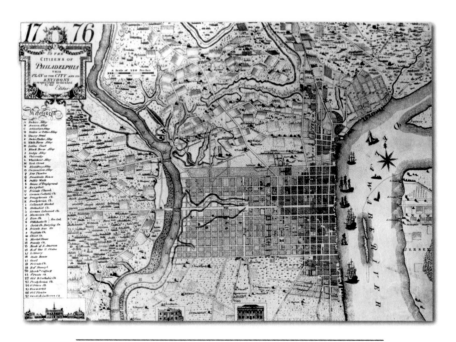

Abigail Adams and her family would move to Philadelphia in 1790. Abigail was forced to leave Philadelphia in 1791, because of illness. She would not return to the city until John Adams was inaugurated as the second president in 1797.

grandfather, John Quincy. After 1791, poor health forced Abigail to spend as much time as possible there. She did not return to Philadelphia during John Adams's two terms as vice president. In the twelve years John served as vice president and then president, Abigail and John Adams once again spent much time apart.

During his second term as president, George Washington made plans to retire. Martha Washington hinted of this to John Adams, who immediately knew what it meant for him. He was the most like- ly choice to be the next president. When Washington left office in 1796, there was a bitter contest for the presiden- cy between John Adams and Thomas Jefferson. Although Adams won by three votes, Jefferson was elected vice president. "I never wanted your advice and assistance more in my life," John wrote to his wife.

President John Adams was inaugu- rated at Congress Hall in Philadelphia on March 4, 1797. People believed that Abigail had more influence on the pres- ident than she had. If someone wanted a position in government, they often wrote directly to her. She could not help them. She was mainly John's sound- ing board, and the only person in whom he could confide.

Once again, Abigail and John Adams had to worry

John Adams, pictured above, had spent his life- time in public service, but many were afraid he couldn't follow the more popular Washington.

This is a photograph of the Historic Congress Hall in Philadelphia, Pennsylvania.

about finances and appearances. They had to live on twenty-five thousand dollars, the same annual salary that John had received from Congress for the past eight years. In spite of inflation, Congress refused to raise the salaries of the president and vice president. It would be very difficult for John Adams to afford a house that suited a man in his position, in addition to the couple's cost of official entertaining. Yet Abigail managed to plan dinner parties and organize a staff of servants and cooks as smoothly as she had managed farmhands and tenants.

In addition to performing her practical duties, Abigail Adams worried about the heavy responsibilities that had been placed on her husband's shoulders. She hoped that he might "be enabled to discharge them with honor to yourself, with justice and impartiality to your country, and with satisfaction to this great people..."

In 1800, the nation's capital was moved again, this time to Washington, D.C. Abigail Adams, who had returned to Quincy to recover her health, rejoined her husband there at the end of the year. The President's House was nearly completed. Many years later, it would

The White House, in Washington, D.C., took a long time to complete. Construction began in October 1792. Although President Washington oversaw the construction of the house, he never lived in it. It was not until 1800, when the White House was nearly completed, that its first residents, President John Adams and his wife, Abigail, moved in.

become known as the White House. Abigail Adams liked the house and its surroundings, but soon found that it was difficult to manage. In a letter to Nabby, she wrote, "The house is upon a grand and superb scale, requiring about thirty servants to attend and keep the apartments in proper order...an establishment very ill proportioned to the President's salary."

It was expensive to keep the many rooms lit, and there was a shortage of wood to keep the fires burning. What little could be found was used in fires to dry the walls before the Adamses came home. They had to resort to the use of coal, which was costly. The house, large as it was, also lacked bells with which Abigail Adams could summon the servants.

John Adams's presidency was not always a popular one, especially in comparison to that of George Washington's. Washington had been a hero of the Revolution. As commander in chief of the American army, Washington led his men to victory with courage and military skill. He was unanimously voted president and even reelected for a second term.

In contrast, John Adams's presidency began with a crisis in foreign affairs. The new leaders of France did not approve of Adams's election and ordered that

This painting by Gordon Phillips shows Abigail Adams and her granddaughter Susanna supervising the hanging of the laundry in the east room of the White House. Historians are not sure if this scene ever occurred, but it is true that life in the White House was much different in Abigail's time than it is today.

American ships be captured, their cargoes confiscated, or seized. They also expelled the American minister to France. John had to take measures to avoid a war.

These were troublesome times, but luckily John Adams had an intelligent partner with whom to discuss his positions on issues. Abigail Adams listened and offered advice. She even sent letters to newspaper editors supporting her husband's policies. As always, Abigail supported him in action and in spirit.

9. Abigail's Revolutionary Ideas

Abigail Adams's ideas sprang from the same soil that nourished the Revolutionary movement. In the 1700s, many of the community leaders and ministers supported the patriots' cause. They believed that men had God-given rights, such as freedom of speech, and that if they were oppressed they had the God-given right to rebel. Abigail Adams was a devoted Christian and these religious arguments helped to strengthen her patriotism.

Abigail Adams also studied history for lessons that could be applied to the present. The writings of historians such as Catherine Macaulay held warnings for the new nation of the abuses of public officials and the loss of liberty of ordinary citizens. Abigail Adams was interested in Macaulay for another reason: She admired exceptional women and their work. Macaulay was a celebrated English historian who had written the *History of England*. "One of my own Sex so eminent in a tract so uncommon naturally raises my curiosity..." Abigail Adams wrote. Abigail did not hesitate to write to her.

This painting of Mary Wollstonecraft Godwin was created after the portrait by J. Opie. Godwin was one of the leading writers and activists for the rights of women. Abigail was influenced by thinkers such as Godwin and persuaded her husband to reconsider the role of women in the new United States.

Mary Wollstonecraft Godwin was another writer whom Abigail Adams admired. Although Abigail Adams believed that an education could improve women's traditional roles in the home, Wollstonecraft went further. In her book, *A Vindication of the Rights of Women*, she wrote that women and men should receive an equal education. In those days, this was an extreme idea.

Abigail Adams and other women of the eighteenth century had reason to be unhappy with their social condition. Women in colonial times did not enjoy many of

This hand-colored woodcut by A. Forestier, from the 1700s, shows well-to-do ladies and gentlemen having tea. A large part of the job for wives of important men was to entertain. Abigail Adams spent most of her time as first lady seeing visitors who hoped she would have some influence over her husband's decisions.

the rights that men did. They were not entitled to an education. They were not allowed to vote. Only men participated in politics. After marriage, a man had control of his wife's property. A woman did not even have rights over her own children. Abigail Adams hoped that the Revolution would bring changes to improve the situation of American women, as well as American men.

Abigail Adams argued women's causes to the man on whom she exerted the most influence, her husband. She asked him to "remember the Ladies," and to "Remember all Men would be tyrants if they could. If perticuliar care and attention is not paid to the Laidies we are determined to foment a Rebelion, and will not hold ourselves bound by any Laws in which we have no voice, or Representation."

Although women's rights were not foremost in John Adams's mind, his wife had a real influence on him, as can be seen in his letter to Brigadier General Joseph Palmer. "Shall we say, that every Individual of the Community, old and young, male and female, as well as rich and poor, must consent...to every act of Legislation?" To his wife, he jokingly compared her arguments to the grievances of Indians and Negroes: "But your Letter was the first Intimation that another Tribe more numerous and powerfull than all the rest were grown discontented. —This is rather too coarse a Compliment but you are so saucy, I wont blot it out."

Dissatisfied with his response, Abigail Adams

Braintree March 31 1776

I wish you would ever write me a letter half as long
as I write you; and tell me if you may where your fleet are
gone! what sort of Defence Virginia can make against our
common Enemy! Whether it is so situated as to make an able
Defence! are not the Gentery Lords & the common people
vassals, are they not like the uncivilized vatives Brittain
represents us to be? I hope their Rifel Men who have
shewen themselves very savage & even Blood thirsty; are not
a Specimen of the Generality of the people

I am willing to allow
the Colony Great merrit for having produced a Washington
but they have been shamefully hazard by a number

I have sometimes been ready
to think that the passion for Liberty cannot be Eaquelly
Strong in the Breasts of those who have been accustomed to
deprive their fellow Creatures of theirs. Of this I am certain
that it is not founded upon that Generous & christian principal
of doing to others as we would that others should do un
to us —

Do not you want to see Boston;
I am fearfull of the small pox, or I should have been in before
this time. I got my Brother to go to our House & see what state
it was in, & find it has been occupied by one of the Doctors of
a Regiment, very dirty, but no other Damage has been done to
it the few things which were left in it are all gone Cranch has
the key which he never delivers up, I have wrote to him for it
& am determined to get it cleand as soon as possible & shut it
up — I looke upon it a new acquisition of property, a property
which one month ago I did not value at a single shilling, and
could with pleasure have seen it in flames

The Town in General is left in
a better state than we expected, more oweing to a percipitate
flight than any regard to the inhabitants, tho some individuals
discoverd a sense of honour & justice & have left the rent of the
Houses in which they were, for the owners & the furniture
unhurt, or if damaged sufficient to make it good
the Ravages — others have committed abomina
and the furniture. the Mansion House of your President is safe
un hurt while

pushed further: "I can not say that I think you very generous to the Ladies, for whilst you are proclaiming
peace and good will to Men, Emancipating all nations,
you insist upon retaining an absolute power over
Wives. But you must remember that Arbit[r]ary power
is like most other things which are very hard, very
liable to be broken—and notwithstanding all your wise
Laws and Maxims we have it in our power not only to
free ourselves but to subdue our Masters, and without
voilence throw both your natural and legal authority at
our feet—" Two centuries later, American women continue to free themselves of men's "natural and legal
authority," as Abigail Adams wisely foretold. Never in
her wildest imagination could she have predicted how
far women would go, but her basic premise was correct.

Because her husband was absent, Abigail Adams
acted quite independently, but her experience was an
exception to the rule. Her relationship with John was
also an unusual one, in which there was a free
exchange of ideas. When John Adams was in Europe for
five years, she argued bitterly to him in letters that it
would be more natural for women to feel indifference
rather than patriotism, since they were mere subjects
to the laws of men and had no voice in government. She
wrote to John, "Yet all History and every age exhibit

This letter from Abigail to John Adams was written on March 31, 1776.
It is the first page of what is possibly her most famous letter, in
which she asks her husband to consider the rights of women
when he frames a new constitution for the United States.

Instances of patriotick virtue in the female Sex; which considering our situation equals the most Heroick of yours." She always considered herself a patriot and saw the American Revolution as "our cause."

Slavery was another emerging social issue in the eighteenth century. In December 1774, George Washington signed the Fairfax Resolves, which barred the importation of slaves, calling it "the wicked, cruel and unnatural trade." Although he had slaves of his own, he recognized the moral offense of the slave trade. Abigail Adams had agreed: "You know my mind upon this Subject. I wish most sincerely there was not a slave in the province." She felt that it was hypocritical for patriots to fight for freedom while "plundering from those who have as good a right to freedom as we have."

"I have sometimes been ready to think that the passion for Liberty cannot be Eaquelly Strong in the Breasts of those who have been accustomed to deprive their fellow Creatures of theirs," she wrote.

Abigail Adams was a product of her times and cannot be described as a supporter of racial equality. That was an idea whose time had not yet come. However, she was consistent in education for everyone. She taught reading and writing to a black servant boy, James, and gave him permission to attend a night school. She said in a speech, "The Boy is a Freeman as much as any of the Young Men, and merely because his Face is Black, is he to be denied instruction, how is he to be qualified to procure a livelihood? Is this the Christian principle of doing to others as we would have others do to us?... I hope we shall all go to Heaven together." Unfortunately, Abigail's neighbors were not as enlightened as she was and they asked her to take him out of the school. They

This depiction of an old-time school in Pennsylvania is from a hand-colored Howard Pyle illustration.

complained that the other boys refused to go to school with a black boy. Still, Abigail defended James's right to an education.

Before leaving for England in 1784, she decided to leave her house in the care of Pheby, a slave whom her father had freed. "The trust is very flattering to her, and both her Husband and she seem pleased with it. I have no doubt of their care and faithfullness, and prefer them to any other family."

In his will, Abigail's father had also left Pheby some money to be paid to her each year during her lifetime. When Pheby married, Abigail Adams let the couple celebrate in her home, "which they did much to their satisfaction."

10. The Legacy of Abigail Adams

When John Adams had sought a wife, he had sought someone who could be a partner in every way. He found this in Abigail Adams, a fiercely independent woman who helped her family through many difficult times. She was an extraordinary woman who lived in extraordinary times.

Abigail Adams proved to be a capable businesswoman. In addition to raising four children, she managed the family home and farm through a bloody war and lengthy separations from her husband.

Although her domestic duties were demanding enough, she also wanted to play a role in the world at large. She believed that women had every ability and right to be involved in matters outside the home. She never limited herself.

Abigail Adams had more opportunities than most women of her day, and she had the courage to take

This is a portrait of Abigail Adams by Gilbert Stuart from 1801. Abigail faced a number of setbacks late in life, including the death of her daughter, Nabby, and constant illnesses which left her bedridden for long periods of time.

advantage of them. She lived in foreign countries, far away from loved ones, where she could observe different cultures and mingle with foreign dignitaries. As wife of a vice president, and later as first lady, she was obliged to play a more public role, planning dinners for important guests.

Above all, Abigail Adams had the courage to think independently. Like most people, she was influenced by the thinking of her contemporaries, but she had the drive and intelligence to find answers to the questions on her mind. She was strong enough to stand by her own values and to make difficult decisions. During her lifetime, education and literacy for women were improving, and legal rights were being established, but for the most part, women's lives were shaped by pregnancy, child rearing, and household labor. In the world of the eighteenth century, she was one of the few voices demanding change.

In spite of this, Abigail Adams could not have envisioned that one day women would have the right to vote. Her revolutionary ideas, almost a century and a half away from female suffrage, or the right to vote, were among those that planted the seeds of a political revolution for women.

Abigail Adams's last years were not always easy. She was greatly saddened by the death of her only daughter, Nabby. She herself was sick much of the time.

Abigail Adams died on October 28, 1818, of typhoid

Abigail Amelia Adams Smith (1765-1813), or Nabby, was the daughter of John and Abigail Adams. Nabby married William Stephens Smith in 1786.

Nabby's death was very hard on Abigail Adams. She was close to her daughter, and her death was a slow and painful one. Nabby developed breast cancer in 1810 and came to her mother's house in 1811 to be cared for by Abigail. While there, Nabby met with the family doctor and decided to have an operation. In that time, surgery was very difficult and painful for the patient. There were no medicines to numb the pain, and the risk of infection was high. Nabby bravely agreed to have the operation despite this. Her breast was removed while she was awake, and this must have been very difficult for everyone present. The operation was successful, but soon the cancer returned and Nabby died in 1812.

Abigail Adams died in her bed in 1818, with her family around her. She had been the wife of one president and the mother of another and was a truly revolutionary woman.

fever, just a few days before her seventy-fourth birthday. She was honored by John, who called her "The dear Partner of my Life for fifty four Years as a Wife and for many years more as a Lover." The couple had been married for fifty-four years.

Her legacy also was maintained through her descendants. As president, John Quincy Adams, whose education she had molded, became known for his diplomacy. He also championed the antislavery cause as a member of the U.S. House of Representatives. His son, Charles Francis Adams, also continued the fight against slavery, as a congressman.

Abigail Adams is buried in a crypt below First Parish Church in Quincy, Massachusetts, next to both her husband and her son John Quincy, underscoring her influence on two American presidents. The church members have preserved the site and made it available to visitors. In nearby Weymouth, the Abigail Adams Historical Society preserves Abigail's birthplace, also open to visitors. Within the Adams National Historic Park, you still can visit John Adams's birthplace, the house where he brought his new bride. In Quincy, you also may visit the house that Abigail bought in 1787, which was home to four generations of Adamses. Nearby is the Abigail Adams Cairn, the hill on which she and John Quincy stood and watched the destruction of the Battle of Bunker Hill. Also in the center of Quincy, there stands a statue of Abigail Adams with her son, commemorating her love for her children.

Abigail Adams is buried alongside her husband, John, and her son John Quincy, in a tomb beneath United First Parish Church in Quincy, Massachusetts. Like their ancestors before them, both Presidents John Adams and John Quincy Adams were lifelong members of the Church.

Timeline

1735	John Adams is born.
1744	Abigail Smith is born.
1764	John and Abigail are married.
1765	The Stamp Act is passed in Parliament.
	John and Abigail's first child, Abigail (Nabby), is born.
1766	Parliament repeals the Stamp Act.
1767	John Quincy Adams is born.
	Parliament passes the Townshend Acts.
1768	Susanna Adams is born.
1770	Charles Adams is born.
	Susanna Adams dies in February.
1772	Thomas Boylston Adams is born.

1773	The Tea Act is passed.
	The Boston Tea Party occurs, Parliament retaliates with the Coercive Acts.
1774	John is a delegate at the First Continental Congress.
1775	Second Continental Congress is in session.
	Revolutionary War begins with the Battle of Lexington and Concord.
1776	Congress signs the Declaration of Independence.
1777	John is elected by Congress to be joint commissioner to France, with Benjamin Franklin and Arthur Lee.
1778	John and John Quincy sail to France.
1779	John and John Quincy return to Boston.
	John is appointed to negotiate peace and trade with Britain.
	John, John Quincy, and Charles sail to France.

1784	Abigail and Nabby sail to England.
1785	The Adamses live in France.
	John Quincy returns to America.
	John, Abigail, and Nabby move to England, after John is named first U.S. minister to Great Britain
1789	John is elected first vice president of the United States.
	George Washington becomes the first president of the United States.
1790	Benjamin Franklin dies.
	John and Abigail move to Philadelphia, the new U.S. capital.
1792	George Washington and John Adams are reelected.
1797	John Adams becomes second president of the United States.
1812	Nabby dies of cancer.
1818	Abigail Adams dies at home in Quincy.
1826	John Adams dies at home in Quincy.

Glossary

acre (AY-ker) A measure of land.

adversity (ad-VER-suh-tee) A state or condition of misfortune.

affable (A-fuh-buhl) Pleasant and at ease while talking to others.

allayed (ah-LAYD) Subdued or reduced in intensity or severity, or relieved.

apprentice (uh-PREN-tis) An inexperienced person learning a skill or a trade.

chintz (CHINTS) A printed fabric from India.

coercive (co-ER-siv) The act of restraining or dominating by force.

confiscated (KON-fih-skayt-id) Seized by public authority.

Congress (KON-gres) The part of the U.S. government that makes laws and is made of the House of Representatives and the Senate. The members of Congress are chosen by the people of each state.

conservative (kun-SER-vuh-tiv) Favoring a policy of keeping things as they are.

constitution (kahn-stih-TOO-shun) The basic rules by which a country or state is governed.

courtship (KORT-ship) The act of seeking another's affections.

creditors (KREH-dih-turz) The people to whom money or goods are owed.

cynic (SIN-ik) Someone who always finds fault with an idea or proposal.

deficit (DEH-fuh-sit) Something that happens when more money has been spent than has been earned.

dysentery (DIH-sen-ter-ee) A disease marked by severe diarrhea and the passage of mucus and blood.

encroachment (in-KROHCH-ment) The tresspass on or the gradual taking over of the rights or posessions of another.

enlightened (en-LY-tend) Being free from ignorance.

envoy (ON-voy) A messenger or a representative from one government to another.

epoch (EH-pik) An event or time that is the starting point of a new period in history.

formidable (FOR-mih-dah-bul) Causing fear or inspiring awe or wonder.

grievances (GREE-vints-ez) Complaints against some cause of distress.

intrepid (in-TREH-pid) Having no reservations, fearless.

lenient (LEE-nee-ent) Of mild or tolerant disposition, or indulgent.

liable (LIE-uh-buhl) Exposed to some adverse action.

maxims (MAK-suhmz) General truths, principles, or rules of conduct.

militia (muh-LIH-shuh) A group of people who are trained and ready to fight in an emergency.

musket (MUS-kit) A gun with a long barrel used in battle and hunting.

negotiate (nih-GOH-shee-ayt) To have a discussion for the purpose of settling a disagreement.

patriot (PAY-tree-uht) A person who loves and defends his or her country.

plight (PLYT) An unfortunate, difficult, or precarious situation.

proportion (pruh-POR-shun) A proper or equal share; or relation of two parts to each other.

prosperity (prah-SPEHR-ih-tee) A time of economic well-being or success.

Puritans (PYUR-ih-tinz) People in the 1500s and 1600s who belonged to the Protestant religion.

quenched (KWENCHT) To have put out or extinguished something, such as a flame.

reinforcements (ree-in-FORS-ments) Things that strengthen, such as additional troops or ships.

rheumatism (ROO-muh-tih-zem) A medical condition involving pain in the muscles or joints.

satirist (SA-tuh-rist) A writer of a literary work that pokes fun at human nature.

sovereignty (SAH-ver-en-tee) Supreme rule or power.

subdue (sub-DOO) To conquer or bring under control.

suitor (SOO-ter) Someone seeking to marry a woman.

turbulent (her-BYUH-lent) Causing great violence or unrest.

upheaval (up-HEE-vuhl) An instance of radical change or disorder.

Additional Resources

To learn more about Abigail Adams, check out the following books and Web sites:

Books

Bober, Natalie S. *Abigail Adams: Witness to a Revolution*. New York, NY: Aladdin Paperbacks, 1998.

Ferris, Jeri Chase, and Elen Beier. *Remember the Ladies: A Story About Abigail Adams*. New York, NY: Carolrhoda Books, 2000.

Wagoner, Jean Brown. *Abigail Adams: Girl of Colonial Days.* New York, NY: Aladdin Paperbacks, 1992.

Web Sites

www.firstladies.org/

www.masshist.org/adams.html

Bibliography

Butterfield, L.H., et. al., eds. *The Book of Abigail and John: Selected Letters of the Adams Family 1762–1784.* Cambridge, MA: Harvard University Press, 1975,

Cappon, Lester J., ed. *The Adams-Jefferson Letters. 2 vols.* Chapel Hill, NC: The University of North Carolina Press, 1959.

DePauw, Linda Grant. *Remember the Ladies.* New York: Viking Press, 1976.

Gelles, Edith B. *Portia: The World of Abigail Adams.* Bloomington, Indiana: University of Indiana Press, 1992.

Langguth, A.J. *Patriots: The Men Who Started the American Revolution.* New York: Touchstone Books, 1989.

Levin, Phyllis Lee. *Abigail Adams: A Biography.* New York: St. Martin's Press, 1987.

Mitchell, Stewart, ed. *New Letters of Abigail Adams.* Boston: Houghton Mifflin Company, 1947.

Ryerson, Richard Alan, et. al., eds. *The Adams Papers: Adams Family Correspondence.* Vols. 5-6. Cambridge, MA: Harvard University Press, 1993.

Withey, Lynne. *Dearest Friend: A Life of Abigail Adams.* New York: Free Press, 1981.

Index

About the Author

Jacqueline Ching is a writer and editor based in New York City. She has written for *Newsweek* and the *Seattle Times*. In fiction, she has written for DC Comics. Her interest in history and the issue of women's rights led her to Abigail Adams.

About the Consultant

Hope Paterson is part of the Abigail Adams Historical Society and volunteers as the curator of the Birthplace of Abigail Smith Adams located at North and Norton Streets in Weymouth, Massachusetts. She was kind enough to give the editor a tour of the house and to share her knowledge of the Adams family and colonial history throughout the process of creating this book.

Credits

Photo Credits

P. 4 © New York State Historical Association, Cooperstown, New York; pp. 6, 28, 56, 61, 98 © U.S. Dept. of the Interior, National Park Service, Adams National Historical Park; pp. 7, 12, 19, 20, 23, 24, 54, 70, 90 courtesy of the Massachusetts Historical Society; pp. 8, 30 © A.G.K., Berlin/SuperStock; pp. 10, 11,18, 22, 39, 50, 53, 55, 65 Bottom, 68, 75, 87, 88, 93, 94, 99 © North Wind Picture Archives; pp. 14, 47 © Joseph Sohm; Visions of America/CORBIS; pp. 26, 33, 59, 62, 66, 80 courtesy of Map Division, The New York Public Library, Astor, Lenox and Tilden Foundations; pp. 29, 35, 37, 41, 48, 78, 79 © Bettmann/CORBIS; pp. 32 © Archivo Iconografico, S.A./CORBIS; pp. 34, 42, 65 Top © CORBIS; pp. 43, 45 © Francis G. Mayer/CORBIS; p. 69 © Charles E. Rotkin/COR-BIS; p. 71 © Burstein Collection/COR; p. 73 © London Aerial Photo Library/CORBIS; p. 76 Bequest of Mrs. Benjamin Ogle Tayloe; Collection of The Corcoran Gallery of Art/CORBIS; p. 77 © Collection of the New-York Historical Society; p. 81, 97 © Archive Photos; p. 82 © Mark Gibson/CORBIS; p. 83 © CORBIS-BETTMANN; p. 84 © White House Collection, courtesy White House Historical Association.

Book Design
Laura Murawski

Layout Designer
Corinne Jacob

Project Editor
Joanne Randolph